SO-DTD-214

# TAIWAN
*Beautiful Island*

# TAIWAN–
## Beautiful Island

## Jo Neher Watters

*An Exposition-Banner Book*

EXPOSITION PRESS
NEW YORK

*Dedicated to*

*friends in Taiwan*

*and my husband,*

*who made this book possible*

EXPOSITION PRESS, INC.

50 Jericho Turnpike, Jericho, New York 11753

FIRST EDITION

LIBRARY OF CONGRESS CATALOG CARD NUMBER: 72-90070

SBN 0-682-47572-6

# CONTENTS

# TAIWAN
*Beautiful Island*

# 1

# BACKGROUND

## Legend of Formation

Supposedly, thousands of years ago some dragons, who lived under a river in China, became restless and decided to go out and explore other parts of the world. They swam down the river and soon found themselves out in the big ocean. They had never had so much room in which to play so they played tag, swam races, and chased each other. In fact, they were so active that they stirred up huge boulders from the bottom of the ocean. Then later when they stopped to rest, the big rocks all settled down in one place, and—there was a new island!

Even today, some people who live on the island of Taiwan, or Formosa, say that the dragons still live down in the ocean near their island. They say that the small earthquakes that shake the island almost every day are caused by the dragons playing too vigorously and bumping the island with their tails. One reason no one worries about the many little earthquakes is that they know the dragons are just having fun.

## Discovery and History

Almost five hundred years ago (A.D. 1400-1500), some Portuguese men, sailing down the coast of China, saw an island that they didn't know existed. As they sailed closer to look at the beautiful green mountains rising above the tall, straight, white cliffs jutting out of the deep blue ocean, they said quietly to each other, "This is the most beautiful land we have ever seen!"

One man suggested, "This must be a new island, and we found it! Let's name it!"

Another ventured, "I think we should call it 'Ihla Formosa' because that is exactly what it is—beautiful island!" The others enthusiastically agreed, and for over four hundred years the island was known only as Formosa.

The sailors went home with such exciting and glowing stories about the beautiful new island they had discovered that many people went there to establish homes. But, unknown to them, Chinese had been exploring for gold on the island fifty years before Columbus discovered America. Several tribes of South Sea Islanders were also roaming the island. Encounters with these original inhabitants, and struggles with undeveloped land, eventually made it impossible for the Portuguese to keep the island for themselves.

Almost one hundred years after the Portuguese found the island, some Chinese sailors approached it from the opposite western side and saw what they thought were rows and rows of terraces, like huge stepping-stones, rising up from the water's edge. One man shouted, "Taiwan! Taiwan!" which literally means "terraced bay." The word was very descriptive and, thinking they had discovered the island, they decided to name it Taiwan. So today the island is called either Formosa or Taiwan. Most of the world refers to it as Formosa, but the people who live there call it Taiwan.

Since the Portuguese first found the island, it has been ruled, attacked, or invaded by seven different nations. The Dutch settled there in 1624, and a couple of years later the Spanish came. By 1641 the Dutch had driven the Spanish out, and in 1661 the Chinese invaded the island, although their rule wasn't established until 1683. It wasn't until 1885 that Taiwan became a province of China. During the next ten years it was attacked by French warships, and in 1894 it was ceded to Japan as a spoil of the first Sino-Japanese war.

The next fifty years were dotted with uprisings as the inhabitants resisted the Japanese rule. Taiwan was also invaded by American and German soldiers, but in 1945, following World War II, Japan returned Taiwan, as an instrument of surrender, to the Republic of China. In 1949 the capital of Nationalist China (as opposed to mainland China, which is under Communist control) was moved to Taiwan. Taipei, the largest city on the island and the capital of the province, was named the capital of the Republic of China, and General Chiang Kai-shek became its first president.

## Geography

Some people think Taiwan is shaped like a pea pod or a tobacco leaf, but the Chinese who live there say it is shaped like a banana. If you look at the map, you can see it resembles all of them. It isn't very large—only 244 miles long and 60 to 90 miles wide. Missouri is four times as large and Texas is fifteen times as large. Taiwan Province consists of seventy-eight islands. Fourteen of these are very near the west-southwest edge of Taiwan island and are part of the Taiwan group. Farther off the western edge of Taiwan is a group of sixty-four tiny islands called the "Penghus" or "Pescadores," which means "fisherman."

The Tropic of Cancer cuts through the center of the island from east to west. This makes the weather subtropical. The summers are long and humid with an average temperature of 80° F. The weather is so damp that if you leave your shoes in the closet for several days, green mold will grow on them. The winters are only two months long and never very cold, although they seem cold because the air is so damp. Sometimes there is snow on the mountain peaks, but when there is, it is so unusual that the newspapers print stories about it.

Every summer and autumn, typhoons (hurricanes) bring strong winds and rain sweeping over the island. Usually the typhoon rains are more helpful than damaging, but once in awhile they are so strong they ruin crops and houses.

Mountains cover the eastern two-thirds of the island. Some of the highest peaks are between 12,000 and 13,000 feet. It is from some of these high peaks along the east coast that the sharpest, steepest, white cliffs in the world drop down into the dark blue Pacific ocean.

Because the mountains are high and the island is small, the rivers are short and swift. Ships can't travel on them, but they are useful for generating electricity and for irrigating farmers."

At the foot of the mountain range, rich, fertile plains slope off to the west. This productive farmland makes up only one-fourth of the island. However, the rich land, warm climate, and plentiful rainfall make Taiwan the "land of farmland.

### Government

The guiding principles of free Chinese government were laid down by Dr. Sun Yat-sen, the Republic's founding father, who guided China after the revolution of October 10, 1911, until his death in 1925. His system is still followed, and provides for government of the people, by the people, and for the people. The written Constitution assures democratic rule and extensive civil rights.

The structure of the national government follows the five-power system. Under the president are five *yuans* (branches of government): executive, legislative, judicial, control, and examination.

The president and vice-president are elected for six-year terms by the National Assembly, which is chosen by popular vote of the people. The two-term limit has been waived for the period of the Communist rebellion.

The executive *yuan* resembles the cabinet of Western countries. The executive yuan president (prime minister) is nominated and appointed by the president of the Republic with the consent of the legislative *yuan*. The deputy prime minister and ministers are appointed by the president of the Republic upon the recommendation of the prime minister. The executive *yuan* is responsible to the president of the Republic. Within the *yuan* are eight ministers (interior, foreign affairs, national defense, finance, education, justice, economic affairs, and communications), two commissions (Mongolian and Tibetan Affairs and Overseas Chinese Affairs), and three offices (Information, Comptroller General and Personnel Administration).

The legislative *yuan* makes the laws. There are four hundred forty-six members elected by direct vote of the people.

The control *yuan*, with seventy-three members, has the power of consent, impeachment, censure, and audit.

Under the judicial *yuan* are the Council of Grand Justices, the Supreme Court, the Administrative Court, and the Committee on the Discipline of Public Functionaries.

The examination *yuan* supervises the ministries of examination and personnel. It safeguards and administers a civil service that employs people of merit for government offices.

There are three main political parties that enjoy equal legal status.

The Kuomintang is the oldest party and has dominated politics since the founding of the Republic. Chiang Kai-shek succeeded Dr. Sun as leader of the Kuomintang.

The Young China party was founded in 1923, and the Democratic Socialist party was established in 1932. Even though they are minority parties, they hold twenty-one seats in the legislative *yuan* and eight in the control *yuan*.

Civil rights guaranteed under the constitution are freedom of person, domicile, speech, and religion. The people are free to assemble and criticize the government. They have the right to work, to own property, to go where and when they please, to petition or file complaints against the government, and to receive compensation if unlawfully sentenced. They enjoy the rights of election, recall, initiative and referendum.

The constitution guarantees equality for all, and to make sure that equality is carried out, women are guaranteed 10 percent of elective offices.

# 2

# RESOURCES

## Trees

More than one half of the island is covered with commercially valuable trees. More than two hundred kinds of trees are native to the island, but the most useful and abundant are spruce, fir, yellow and red cypress, hemlock, camphor, and bamboo. Because timber is the island's largest natural resource, the government sponsors a reforestation program to conserve the supply of trees. Their reforestation process of cutting all of the trees in one area and replacing them immediately with seedlings has given the mountainsides the appearance of a patchwork quilt with each patch having its own distinctive size, shape, type of tree, and color.

Campor trees grow in many parts of the world, but Taiwan furnishes most of the camphor wood that is used for making furniture. Camphor wood has a characteristic odor that repels insects and worms that bore into many other woods. The wood is soft enough to be easily hand-carved, so it is used to make decorative chests for storing furs and woolens. Burning camphor has a pungent, pleasant odor and gives the same taste to food steeped in the smoke.

Bamboo grows so easily and rapidly that it is very important for domestic use. It will grow equally well in small bunches or in large forests. The wood is strong, flexible, and lightweight. Some is so hard it can be used like flintstone, to strike a spark. The jointed, hollow stems may grow as tall as one hundred feet and as thick as twelve inches. Near every farmhouse is a clump of bamboo to give shade from the hot sun, to provide building and fence material, and to supply food.

New bamboo sprouts that shoot up through the ground are delicious and are used in almost every Chinese vegetable dish. In fact, they are so popular, even with foreigners, that they are being canned for export.

Around every building under construction is a network of bamboo poles that have been lashed together with native hemp ropes. This makes a scaffolding over which the workmen scamper easily, quickly, and safely. In mountainous areas, suspension bridges are built in a similar fashion.

Other uses for bamboo include making lightweight, durable, inexpensive furniture; weaving baskets, chair seats, and beds from the outer peeling stripped off the stems; making steamers that give a special flavor to Chinese foods; manufacturing personal ornaments such as earrings, brooches, and hair clasps from the fine inner peelings; and grinding parts of the stem joints for medications. Bamboo is more valuable for domestic use than for export.

Although the other woods are used for interior finishings and furniture, they are most valuable as exports.

### Minerals

Coal, which is necessary for industrial growth, is Taiwan's most important ore. However, the mining of coal has not been able to keep up with the demand for it, so some has had to be imported. Recently, natural gas was discovered under the surface of the island, which has decreased some of the need for imported coal. Oil has also been discovered, but not in usable amounts.

Huge deposits of marble are being mined. White marble is the most abundant and is used in the construction of buildings. Green, black, and gray varieties add unique and interesting decorative touches. Even though marble is heavy, it is sculptured and ground into many household items such as lamps, vases, parts of furniture, and eating utensils.

Some of the world's largest coral deposits are off the coast of Taiwan, and large deposits of jade have been discovered on the island. Gold, silver, and copper mines furnish enough precious metals to combine with the coral and jade to make Taiwan jewelry, which is popular in many countries.

## Wildlife

Small deer, wild goats, and wild pigs roam over the mountains. They are all hunted for food, but the wild pig (wild boar) is probably the favorite. It is always offered as a choice of meats at the popular Mongolian barbecues.

Thirty-seven different kinds of snakes, twelve of which are poisonous, live on the island. Skins of the large snakes are treated, dried, and often dyed before being offered for sale. Snake skins are very popular among tourists who have them made into shoes, purses, and belts.

Snake meat is often referred to as a delicious luxury food. There are shops in which a person can select a live snake from a cage and wait while it is prepared for him to eat. However, even though the meat is declared to be delicious by those who eat it, it is not really popular. A type of medicine, popular among the Taiwanese people, is also made from a species of snake.

Monkeys live and play in the trees of the forests, but instead of being a resource, they are often pests. At night they steal the farmer's crops, and they are so clever and evasive that they are hard to control. They especially like to steal bananas from the trees about the time the fruit is ready to harvest. Some farmers have been fairly successful in controlling the monkeys by keeping a "feeding ground" for them well supplied with food. Clever monkeys!!

## Flowers

An exciting array of colorful wild flowers add to the beauty as well as to the economy of the island. Flowers growing in abundance on the island are similar to those grown in the southern part of the United States. The huge, bright pink azaleas are so brilliant and plentiful that they have been named the "Formosa" azalea. Early in the spring, the air is full of perfume from the lovely, white, waxy lillies. In the fall the bright red poinsettias (Christmas flower) grow as tall as the houses.

When the rhododendrons are in bloom, the sides of the mountains appear to be covered with fluffy pink and white blankets. In the southern part of the island, orchids hang from trees above the fern-covered earth. Recently, horticulturists on the island have developed a rose that grows easily, remains fresh for a long time, and looks almost too perfect to be real. Cut flowers are for sale in every marketplace and along the streets, and they are very inexpensive. Every home is decorated with fresh flowers, and flower arranging is an art all girls learn when they are young. Because of the great variety and profusion of flowers, horticulture is becoming important to Taiwan. The lotus, or water lily, is lovely and is representative of China, but it was originally used for food. Its tuberous roots and nutlike seeds are still important vegetables, both for the Chinese and for export. Hibiscus is another beautiful flower that is native to China, and its buds are used for seasoning curries.

## Agriculture

Three-fourths of the island of Taiwan consists of lovely, tree-covered mountains, which leaves only one-fourth usable for farming. However, enough food is grown in this small area to feed the 14,000,000 people who live on the island and be an important export item.

In 1949 the government began a program by which each farmer could eventually own the land on which he lived. The land had previously been held by the government or wealthy landowners. By 1968 almost all of the farmers owned their farms.

In addition to owning their own farms, the farmers are learning more scientific methods of farming, and have harnessed the fast-moving streams to irrigate their land. They now use chemical fertilizers that are made on the island, and are studying the control of pests and plant diseases. Consequently, the yield of crops has doubled, and in some cases, tripled. One plot of ground is often used for three crops in one year.

Teams of experts are going to other countries with similar climates to assist in their agricultural programs.

## Water Buffalo

On Taiwan the water buffalo is the beast of burden. He is very slow and clumsy but strong and gentle. He can pull crude plows through the heavy mud of rice paddies, drag huge bundles of logs, or tug heavily loaded carts. Every farmer owns at least one water buffalo.

Because the water buffalo are very gentle, they may be cared for by children. After the water buffalo has finished a hard day's work, children take him to a pond or to the edge of the river for cleaning and relaxation. If the water is deep enough, he wades slowly into the water until only his nose is sticking out. If the water is shallow, he will lie down and roll over and over wallowing in the mud and water. He likes to soak a long time, so the children play nearby until time to go home. He is always reluctant to leave the nice cool water, so the children have to call repeatedly, scream at him, beg and prod him to move out. Once out of the water, he stands quietly and contentedly while the children scrub him and throw water over him. This chore finished, they climb on his back to ride and giggle as he plods slowly home through the dusk. The water buffalo is a friend of the family as well as the beast of burden.

## Rice

Rice is the staple food of Taiwan. Each person eats two or three bowls of rice with each meal. An adult eats at least thirty pounds of rice each month.

The warm climate and rich soil make it possible to raise two crops of rice each year. With new methods and fertilizers, there is four times more rice grown today in one year than could be grown in one year twenty-five years ago. Rice has become one of Taiwan's main exports.

In the marketplaces there are many kinds of rice displayed in large gunnysacks. A good cook knows exactly the kind of rice best suited for the food she plans to prepare, and a house-wife often has several kinds available.

Even with new methods and machines, much of the work of growing and harvesting rice is done by hand. The seed is planted very thickly in small beds and when the plants are six to eight inches tall, the whole family helps transplant them into the rice paddies.

Rice paddies are plots of ground surrounded by dykes, or walls, of mud and rock so water can be held inside. The ground is prepared for the rice plants by breaking it up with a crude plow usually pulled by a water buffalo. Next it is broken into smaller clods and smoothed with a harrow before it is flooded with water to a depth of six to eight inches. The men, women, and children who transplant the rice wear big hats and long sleeves to protect themselves from the hot sun and the mosquitoes. They place plants in a basket strapped to their backs and wade into the water and mud where they place each little plant in the mud in straight rows. The plants are placed so that you look down straight rows in any direction. The paddies are kept flooded, to increase the growth of rice and discourage the growth of weeds, until the rice is ready to harvest.

When the rice is ripe, it has heads of grain, like wheat, that turn yellow. When the color begins to change, the paddies are drained and in a few days the rice is cut by hand, tied in bundles, and stacked to dry. After several days in the hot sun, the bundles are carried to the threshing machine, which is usually operated by hand, although motorized threshing machines are becoming popular. As each bundle is held in the machine with the heads against a paddle wheel, the wheel is rotated so the paddles hit the heads of grain and the loose grain falls out and is collected in large baskets. The straw is stacked to dry as it has many uses.

Freshly threshed grain must be spread to dry. For this purpose, a drying yard is prepared near the farmhouse. The selected plot is smoothed, watered, packed down, and then allowed to dry until it is like cement. The fresh grain is piled on this surface in rows several feet apart. As the hot sun shines on the grain, some one, often a child, moves through the rows, constantly turning the grain. An older person follows less often, lifting the rice in scoopfuls and letting it fall as the wind blows out the chaff. Farmers who live near a highway, spread their grain in rows along the edge of the highway so the cars whizzing by help it dry and blow away the chaff. But, however it is done, after the grain is dry and clean, it is ready to take to market or to store for family use.

## Sugar Cane

The climate of southern Taiwan is perfect for growing sugar cane. Sugar was one of the attractions for the Dutch when they occupied the island, and it has been important for nearly four hundred years.

Under an international agreement, Taiwan may export 630,000 tons of sugar each year. This makes Taiwan rank third, after Cuba and Australia in sugar export. Production is controlled by the government-owned Taiwan Sugar Corporation and is the biggest business on the island. Many farmers grow the cane under contract. In addition to sugar, the processing of sugar cane yields molasses, alcohol, yeast, chemicals, pulp for paper, and animal feed. Hog raising in encouraged because food from the sugar cane pulp is cheap and is excellent for the growth and development of pigs.

The biggest buyers of Taiwan sugar are Japan, the United States, South Korea, and the countries of free Southeast Asia.

## Tea

There is an ancient Chinese story about a philosopher who discovered tea. He was making a long journey by foot and became tired and thirsty. So, in true Chinese fashion, he stopped, built a fire and boiled water to purify it before drinking. Then, just as he was ready to drink the hot water, a breeze blew some dried leaves in his cup. The water turned brownish-green, but he was so thirsty he drank it anyway. He found it so delicious he gathered more of the leaves to take home. He may or may not have been the first man to drink tea, but it is known that the culture of tea began in China hundreds of years ago. Taiwan is now the fifth largest exporter of tea in the world.

In Taiwan, offering a glass of hot tea to a visitor is an indispensible part of Chinese hospitality. Every office and business establishment has a "tea girl" who has been hired to keep a glass of fresh tea on every desk, offer tea to visitors as soon as they arrive, and to take care of the tea utensils.

### Vegetables

Next to rice, vegetables make up the most important food in Taiwan. There is an abundant supply of green beans, broccoli, corn, several kinds of cabbage, mushrooms, and many others. Since there is a constantly producing vegetable crop, the Chinese people use only fresh vegetables. Bamboo shoots, bean sprouts, mushrooms, and water chestnuts are special Chinese vegetables and they are the real aristocrats of the vegetable kingdom. Asparagus is relatively new to Taiwan, but it grows luxuriantly and is in great demand.

Ginger, although not really a vegetable, is cooked with all other dishes for seasoning. The cut-up root of ginger gives a fresh, delicious flavor to any food. However, in bite-sized pieces, it is very pungent. Ginger root, preserved in syrup, candied, or pickled in brine, is used as a condiment with Eastern or Western dishes.

Sweet potatoes are plentiful and farmers depend on them

as the main source of food for pigs. They grow so easily and are so plentiful that they are very inexpensive. People in rural areas eat them in place of rice because they are so cheap. In the cities, steamed sweet potatoes are a delicacy. In the evenings a sweet-potato vendor pushes his cart around neighborhoods calling, "*Yaki-imo! Yaki-imo!*" which advertises his baked potatoes. People buy the roasted potatoes to eat as they sit around relaxing and visiting. Taiwan sweet potatoes are very light yellow, almost white in color.

Peanuts are grown to make peanut oil, which is the main cooking oil used in Chinese cooking. Peanuts are also roasted, or soaked in salt water and steamed, to be eaten as snacks. In front of every theatre are vendors selling hot, salted peanuts.

### *Fruit*

Fresh fruit is always available and is an important part of the diet. Much of the fruit is exported, so it has to be harvested just before it ripens. However, the fruit eaten on the island is field ripened and very sweet, juicy, and tasty.

Pineapple allowed to ripen in the field is especially sweet and juicy. In the spring when it is plentiful, carts piled high with the greenish-brown pineapples are on every street corner in every neighborhood. When a customer selects a pineapple, the vendor prepares it while he waits. It is a breathtaking sight to watch as the vendor takes the pineapple in one hand, a very large sharp knife in the other, and juggles the pineapple up and down and around as he slashes away the tough peeling. In less than a minute he covers the peeled pineapple with a paper napkin and in a flourish hands it to the purchaser who carries it home, dripping sweet, sticky juice every step of the way—unless he remembered to bring a pan to carry it in. The most delicious breakfast you ever tasted!

Bananas grow in southern Taiwan in large orchards, in small orchards, in farmyards, and along highways. Bananas like the damp, warm atmosphere and grow with very little attention. Gentle breezes make the broad green leaves sway like huge, slow-moving fans. Visitors, seeing banana trees for the first time are intrigued with the large bunches of bright green bananas with their tips pointing skyward.

When bananas are mature, they turn yellow very quickly and are soon overripe. So at harvest time, every one works as fast as possible. Bunches of not-quite-ripe bananas are cut from the trees and stacked carefully in piles. Trucks take them to the docks where they are loaded on "banana boats" which take them on their long, slow journey to a foreign land. They travel in refrigerated storage to delay further ripening. Bananas to be eaten on the island are allowed to ripen on the trees which adds to their sweetness.

Other delicious fruits that are too fragile to ship fresh are big, sweet, yellow papayas; red, spiny, sweet lichee nuts; many different kinds of tangerines; smooth, red persimmons that look like big ripe tomatoes; and grapes. Small seedless watermelons, with pink or yellow meat, are dessert favorites any time of the year.

## Livestock

Chinese people eat very little meat, but pork is their favorite. Every farmer has a few pigs to furnish special pork treats for festivals and celebrations. Often small pigs are prepared and roasted whole.

Pigs that are raised for market are kept in sheds and never allowed to root around on the ground. Sheds have cement floors that are scrubbed and washed daily. Near each pig shed is a large outdoor fireplace where all of the pig's food is cooked. Keeping the pigs clean and cooking their food prevents trichinosis, a disease that attacks pigs in other countries but does not exist on Taiwan. A diet of sweet potatoes and sugar cane meal makes the pigs grow rapidly, producing tender, juicy meat and little fat.

Fish is a delightfully fresh favorite food that is prepared and eaten the day it is caught. Some favorite ways of preparing fish are steaming, frying, in soup, and smoked. Camphor-smoked pomfret (a kind of fish) is a very special treat. The very best and freshest fish is often served raw with cold, spiced rice, ginger, and soy sauce. Just ask for *sashimi.*

Near every farmhouse is a small pond or river, which makes ideal conditions for raising ducks or geese, but not chickens. Both ducks and geese are used for food, but ducks are more popular. Duck eggs, which are light blue in color and a little larger than chicken eggs, are used for cooking.

Duck farms are located along rivers. The duck farmer fences in a section of the river by his house where his ducks are allowed to swim and feed. However, when the food becomes scarce, he takes them to other feeding grounds. To do this, he opens a gate or section of the fence and chases the ducks out into the river. Then he gets in a little rowboat and paddles along behind them. He calls to them as he herds them, just like a cowboy herding cattle. The ducks stay close together and obey their "duck boy" as he takes them out in the morning and brings them home at night. It is an interesting sight to see herds of ducks swimming along the rivers.

Taiwan is not a dairy country so the supply of fresh milk is limited. Dried milk is received from other countries, and converted into liquid milk. Soy bean "milk" is also available. To make it the soy beans are soaked, treated, ground, and strained. The "milk" is tasty and nutritious. Doctors in many countries recommend the use of soy bean "milk."

The Taiwan government believes that milk is good for its people so they encourage farmers to buy cattle. Cows and bulls have been imported from dairy countries to get a good strain of dairy cows started in Taiwan. Farmers have organized themselves into groups to study and experiment with different breeds of dairy cows. They are learning to treat the milk to keep it safe to drink, and have set up controls for distribution and pricing of milk. They are also planning future markets, such as ice cream production.

## Imports—Exports

Imports are mainly raw materials and tools. Exports are mainly manufactured products, food, and textiles.

With the rapid growth of Taiwan's exports, and increased personal income, the future of her economy seems good.

With Taiwan securing its place in world affairs, it is a country demanding the attention and study of the world. Even individual lives are enriched by studying and understanding another culture.

## Transportation

Taiwan has over 10,000 miles of highways, 2,400 miles of railroads, and an international airport where the latest jets can land.

One main highway leads along the western coast, through villages and farmlands. Here the people are busy and peaceful. Women can be seen washing their clothes in swift-moving, rock-bottomed streams while children play nearby. This route offers an opportunity to see rice paddies being planted and harvested.

The other main highway follows the eastern coast, cutting

through mountains and winding through breathtakingly beautiful Toroko Gorge. It passes along cliffs, over bridges, and through tunnels of solid marble. The lush growth of green trees, colorful flowers, and ground shrubs, interrupted by thunderous white sprays of cascading falls, make this one of the most fascinating spots in the world.

Trains carry about 300,000 passengers each day. Beside each seat on the trains, under the window, is a holder for two tea glasses. As soon as the train leaves the station, girls bring kettles of boiling water and offer each passenger a choice of tea bags. Jasmine tea is a favorite of many because of its refreshing flavor and delicate aroma.

Taipei's international airport is new and always busy. It handles nearly fifty flights a day either arriving from or departing to foreign countries. There are also many domestic planes flying to other parts of the island. The airport is a colorful place with people from many countries wearing their native costumes. Even the dreaded task of "going through customs" has been eased by efficient, pleasant, and fast handling of tourists and luggage. China Airlines, the Chinese flag carrier, services the entire Far East.

Bicycles, motorcycles, and automobiles furnish individual transportation anywhere in the island. Motorcycles and automobiles are being assembled in Taiwan from parts shipped in from other countries. Taxis are numerous, small, inexpensive, always available, and are all the same color. People, bicycles, motorcycles, cars, and taxis are creating traffic problems. However, increased education in traffic rules and the construction of new streets and highways, are helping to improve the situation.

# 3

# CULTURE

## Family Life

Hundreds of years before the birth of Christ, a great Chinese philosopher, Confucius, said, "Do not do unto others what you would not have them do unto you." Believing his words, the Chinese have respect for all people. This especially applies to family life. Children may not agree with their parents, but they respect them as their ancestors and the source of their existence. Even today, in a time of great social change in all countries, the Chinese still have a strong sense of family responsibility.

Families have fun together. They visit together and go to movies, amusement parks, the seaside, and restaurants. Parents take very young children wherever they go, so the children learn to enjoy the same things their parents do, and they learn to act in a manner acceptable to all ages. Parents are actively interested in their children's education and welfare. In return, the children believe it is a privilege as well as a duty to care for their parents when they grow old.

## Dress

Clothing in Taiwan is a mixture of traditional Chinese styles and modern Western styles. Children and young people dress just like they do in the United States. Through the first twelve years of school, students wear uniforms to school. The uniforms are usualy white middy blouses and dark skirts for the girls, and sport shirts with short or long pants for the boys. Since the weather is warm most of the year, lightweight clothing is worn.

Most Chinese women wear the *chi pao*, or Chinese style dress. The basic style of the *chi pao* has not changed through the years. It has close, body-hugging lines with a high, close-fitting collar, and slits in the skirt at the knee. In the *chi pao*, the Chinese woman looks very lovely and chic. Modernization has had its effect on the *chi pao* too, and the collars are not as high nor the slits as long as they once were. Older women of a more aristocratic generation remember when social position required collars as high as possible, and the slits in the skirts began at the ankle and went to the knee. This regal appearance has been sacrificed to comfort with a lower, looser collar and short skirts that do not allow such long slits.

Formal gowns today retain a majestic air, with long skirts that feature slits to above the knee, often outlined with beads or braid. The beautiful Chinese silk brocade molded into the form-fitting *chi pao* lends an air of aristocratic elegance to its wearer, even with the "little jacket" effect for air-conditioned rooms.

The everyday working dress is made according to the same pattern, but is looser for comfort and ease of movement, and is made of simple dark cotton.

Men in Taiwan dress just like men do in the United States. They are neat and well-groomed but because of the hot weather they wear sport shirts for all informal occasions.

## Eating Habits

Eating is a very important social custom to Chinese people. They often greet friends by saying, "Have you eaten?" An average home meal consists of a very small amount of meat or fish, a vegetable, soup, and rice. They seldom drink anything with their meals because they drink hot tea often during the day, and to relax before a meal.

Everyone in a Chinese home eats with chopsticks. They are very adaptable and convenient—for anyone who is clever enough to use them! All food is cut into bite-sized pieces before it is cooked so there is no need for a knife at the table.

Chinese, like the people of other nations, have their own rules of etiquette, and the ones concerning eating habits are exacting and strictly practiced. For instance, there is a correct way to eat soup. If the soup is brothlike, with only a few pieces of vegetables or meat in it, the pieces of solid material should be removed and eaten with chopsticks, then the bowl lifted with both hands to the mouth to drink the liquid. If the soup is thick or creamy, it should be eaten with a porcelain spoon. The spoon is shaped like a little flat-bottomed boat, with a short handle on one end, and it is usually decorated with a dainty little flower in the bowl of the spoon and on the handle.

Toothpicks are always available during and after a meal. They may be used at any time, but always behind a hand that is carefully held in front of the mouth to shield it from view.

A formal Chinese dinner is usually served in a restaurant, in a Chinese dining room in a hotel, or in a private club. It may consist of a dozen or more courses. A rule of thumb for estimating the number of courses to serve is: one main dish for each guest, and several appetizer dishes, soups, and desserts. An authentic Chinese dinner is always served at a round table that will seat ten to fourteen persons.

At the table each place is set with a small plate, porcelain spoon, small soup bowl, wine cup, saucer for soy sauce, and a pair of chopsticks. Often with this setting is a decorative little chopstick-holder that resembles a little bridge. When the chopsticks are not in use, they rest across the "bridge," with handles on the table and used ends up in the air. All the dishes are small because only a few bites of food are placed on the individual plates at one time. To keep the plates from looking messy, or to keep flavors from mingling, clean plates are supplied often. The tiny wine glasses are kept filled to use for frequent "toasting."

The seating of guests at a formal dinner is significant. The guest of honor is seated on the north side of the table, or with his back to the wall so he looks into the open room. The host sits opposite him, and other guests are seated with the highest ranking next to the guest of honor. However, when a Western guest is present, a Chinese cohost will sit beside him to assist him and explain the various foods and customs. Chinese are fun-loving people and dinners are an occasion of vivacious conversation and much laughter.

Several cold dishes, or appetizers, are placed on the table just before the guests are seated, and wine cups are filled as soon as everyone is in place. As soon as all glasses are filled, the host raises his glass and says, *Ch'ing* ("please"), to which everyone raises his glass then drinks. Following the toast, the host raises his chopsticks and again says, *Ch'ing* and the guest of honor serves himself and begins to eat. The host serves himself last and eats very little as he is busy watching his guests to be sure they are completely satisfied.

Following the cold dishes, all other courses are served on huge platters, or bowls for soup, one at a time. Each is placed in the center of the table where it remains until it is finished.

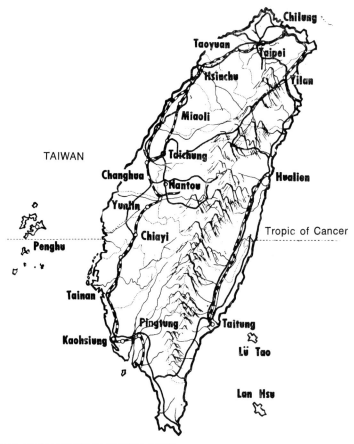

TAIWAN

Chilung
Taoyuan
Taipei
Hsinchu
Yilan
Miaoli
Taichung
Changhua
Nantou
Hualien
Yunlin
Chiayi
Tropic of Cancer
Penghu
Tainan
Pingtung
Taitung
Kaohsiung
Lü Tao
Lan Hsu

The water buffalo is Taiwan's beast of burden. Slow but strong, he is so gentle an animal that he is often entrusted to the care of children. Here he takes a moment's rest during the plowing of a field.

Arable land is not plentiful in Taiwan, and it is, therefore, carefully planned and cultivated. Farms are terraced, as shown, which helps the ground to hold water.

A vegetable farm at the foot of a picturesque mountain. Bamboo shoots, bean sprouts, mushrooms, and water chestnuts are among the vegetables grown on the island.

Rice is the staple food of Taiwan and many people, including children, are engaged in its cultivation. This field is being plowed with the aid of a water buffalo.

Rice being cut and shocked preparatory to drying.

A young bicyclist pauses alongside a field of shocks drying in the sun.

Pork is the favorite meat of the Chinese people. Pigs are carefully raised, kept in clean pens, and fed only fresh cooked food. Trichinosis, a common disease of pigs, does not exist on Taiwan.

One of Taiwan's two main highways winds through the spectacular Toroko Gorge, along cliffs, over bridges, and through tunnels of solid marble.

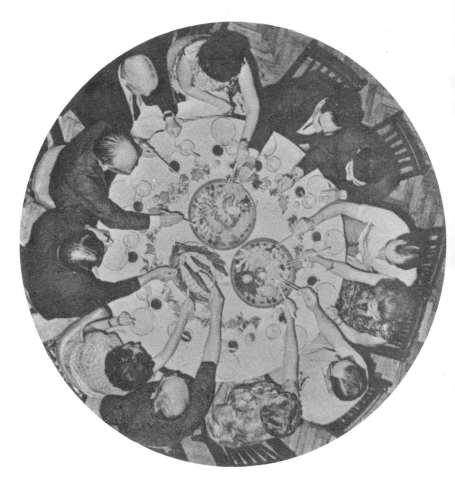

A formal Chinese dinner is usually served at a round table. The guests help themselves with chopsticks from a variety of different dishes.

Taiwan's original inhabitants came from the South Pacific and their descendants, Amis, resemble Polynesians more than Chinese. These Ami girls celebrate the harvest festival in traditional costumes.

The summer season always begins with dragon boat races. These are colorful and exciting, and a drummer stands in the prow beating the stroke on a large drum.

Chinese Opera is a brilliant and inspiring spectacle. The costumes are bright and elaborate and the singers have heavily painted faces and use broad symbolic gestures.

Chinese painting is most distinctive. It is extremely light and delicate, with little perspective. A legend is often included in the paintings in calligraphy (Chinese writing), which is an art in itself.

This giant Buddha is at Changhua in Central Taiwan. It is 72 feet tall. Buddhism, one of the popular religions of Taiwan, is known as a religion of love and peace.

Taiwan students wear uniforms and carry their books in bags slung across their shoulders. Education is free and compulsory through the ninth grade. Most Taiwanese can read and write, and many go on to college.

Name chops have been used for signatures in China since ancient times. Formerly made of precious jade, they are now more often made of ivory, bamboo, soapstone, or metal. This picture shows a variety of chops and how they are used.

A busy street in Taipei, the largest city in Taiwan and the capital of the Republic of China. With over one million inhabitants, the city is busy, noisy, and crowded.

The National Historical Museum in Taipei is an example of typical Chinese architecture. Inside, elaborate displays and exhibits trace the history of China back to ancient times.

A public park in the capital city. The skyline of the city of Taipei can be seen in the background.

Kaoshiung, located at the southern end of the island, is the industrial center of Taiwan and the site of the only oil refinery.

A picturesque and typically oriental zigzag bridge near the busy seaport of Kaoshiung.

Stamp collecting is popular in Taiwan, and there are both local and national philatelic societies. The stamps are artfully designed and are among the world's most beautiful.

The people of Taiwan have a keen interest in games, body building, and all forms of sport. Here the Little League of Taiwan proudly displays their world championship banner.

Then the empty platter is removed and the next course is served. With each course, a pair of large serving chopsticks and several silver spoons are placed on the table beside the platter. Each guest serves himself by reaching with the serving chopsticks, or the spoon to the food in the center of the table, and bringing it to his small plate.

The six or eight hot courses that follow the appetizers consist of seafood, chicken, duck, vegetables, pork, and beef. They may be tantalizingly steamed, fried, roasted, smoked, or prepared in an unusual manner that will stimulate appetites and conversation.

Camphor-smoked duck is steamed until it is tender, then steeped for several minutes in the smoke from burning camphor wood chips, green tea, and sugar. It has a flavor to remember!

Beggar's chicken always brings stories from the guests. It is prepared, stuffed with seasonings, wrapped in leaves, thoroughly covered with mud, and baked over an open fire. To serve it, the mud is cracked away, the leaves opened, and chicken, tender enough to pick off the bones with chopsticks, is presented to the table of guests. It is as delicious as the hobo stories are interesting.

Crisp roast duck that has been steamed, then fried in deep fat until it is a golden brown, is brought to the table to be admired. It is then returned to the kitchen where the crisp brown skin is stripped off and served with a special sauce and tiny, thin, bread sandwiches. When the crisp sandwiches have been eaten, the duck meat is served in succulent, tender chunks. While the meat is being eaten, soup for the next course is made from the leftover duck.

Everyone looks forward to "bomb" soup which is made at the table. Rice has been boiled, dried, and fried until it is very dry and crisp. Then it is broken into pieces and heaped in a large bowl which is placed in the center of the table.

Then a waiter brings a pot of steaming hot shrimp soup and pours it quickly over the rice. As the rice snaps, pops, and crackles, the guests oh, ah, and ooh!

The last of the hot main dishes is always fish, served whole on a large platter. Sometimes it is covered with a sweet and sour sauce, but it is always delicious with whatever sauce is used.

One or two sweet dishes served next may be glutinous sweet rice dumplings; glazed bananas or sweet potatoes so hot that they must be dipped into dishes of water to cool them enough to eat; date cakes; or sweet lotus soup.

To finish the dinner, another hot dish, rice, and soup are served before the final, beautifully arranged platter of fresh fruit is placed in the center of the table for guests to choose their favorites.

## Festivals

Festivals are a vital part of Chinese culture. There are national festival days and individual family festival days. All are important and each is celebrated with special activities and distinctive foods. There are so many festivals that one seems to be celebrated every day. A few of the festivals of national importance may be interesting to you.

### Chinese New Year Festival

The Chinese New Year festival celebrates the beginning of the new year based on the movements of the moon. This is called the lunar calendar. The first day of the lunar year may fall on a different day each year, but it is always between January 21 and February 21.

The New Year festival is the biggest and most widely celebrated of all the festivals. In ancient times the celebration lasted a month, but today the legal period is two days. During the festival all businesses close so the entire attention can be given to celebrations. Family gatherings, accompanied by feasting and exploding firecrackers are the main events.

In preparation for this celebration, sixteen days before the new year, customers pay their bills, and business men close their books for the year. Not only does everyone pay his debts, but he must prepare his own home. Legend says the kitchen god returns to heaven at the end of each year to give his report on the family activities of the past year. To make sure he says only good things, candy is smeared on the mouth of his image to seal his lips, or to let out only sweet words. He is also offered wine in the hope that he will get drunk and forget all the bad things he may have seen. Paper money is burned in front of him so he will be assured of a comfortable journey. Then before he returns on New Year's eve, every member of the family helps clean, repair, or paint the house and place a new kitchen-god image in the kitchen for him to dwell in another year. Then a sumptuous feast is prepared to welcome him home and to show him what a happy, fine, family he lives with.

For New Year's feasts, ordinary food is given special names. The names all have meanings of prosperity and good fortune. Eggs are called "silver nuggets," mushrooms are "opportunities," and chicken is "phoenix."

Traditionally, there are certain things that should be done and others that should not be done on New Year's Day. Ancestors must be honored with red scrolls hanging on the walls asking for happiness, prosperity, and long life. A basket of food is placed in the center of the living room to assure everyone there will be enough to eat during the coming year. Knives and scissors must be hidden so no one will accidentally cut the luck of the new year. Everyone wears his newest and finest clothes to show his intentions to do his best in the new year. Being on one's good behavior shows that one plans to do only good deeds in the year ahead.

### LANTERN FESTIVAL

On the fifteenth day of the new year, the Lantern festival marks the end of the holiday season. The ancient Chinese believed they could see spirits in the sky during the first full moon of the year. The spirits would guide them to prosperity during the coming year. They carried torches and gathered on the highest nearby hill to gaze into the skies to watch for the spirits to appear. To fill their time while waiting, they took rice dumplings filled with sweet or salty pork to munch on. The dumplings were round and filled to look like the moon.

This custom is still followed today, except that the torches have been replaced by lanterns. Years ago someone brought a lantern to the hillside and it was admired so much that the next year others brought lanterns. Very soon there was great competition to see who could make the largest, most beautiful, or most unusual lantern. Then someone began making lanterns to sell and parades were held to display them. Nowadays there is a carnival atmosphere with the parades that show off brightly colored paper lanterns. Lanterns of lifelike animal designs and size, and of make-believe dragons, are trailed through city and neighborhood streets. Eventually the lantern-bearing people assemble on a hill to sit and eat dumplings while gazing into the sky until after midnight.

### DRAGON BOAT FESTIVAL

The dragon boat festival is the biggest event of the summer. On the fifth day of the fifth moon, the summer season begins with dragon boat races. The long, narrow, graceful boats are painted with bright colors and decorated with lion's heads. There is great rivalry between racing teams.

The legend of this festival concerns a scholar who served an emperor about 2000 years ago. When the scholar tried to help the poor people by making suggestions to the emperor, he was sent away. As the emperor continued to ignore him, he became very sad, and he jumped in the river and was drowned. When the poor people who loved him heard about it, they jumped in boats and rushed out to look for him, but they were too late. However, they did throw rice into the water to comfort his spirit. Every year after that, people went out in boats to look for his spirit and drop rice into the water. When they noticed that the rice floated apart and away, they wrapped and tied it in bamboo leaves.

Today the dragon boat races are colorful and exciting, and rice dumplings wrapped in bamboo leaves are sold from carts.

## Moon Festival

Autumn's most colorful festival is the Moon, or Harvest, festival. It falls on the fifteenth day of the eighth month because the moon is believed to be its brightest at that time, and the earth god is thanked for the harvest. Since this is also called the Moon festival, it is interesting to know some of the beliefs about the moon.

There is a legend that explains why the moon is considered to be the symbol of femininity. Beautiful Chang-O, who lived about 2000 B.C., is now supposed to live on the moon. She was very lovely and wanted to remain beautiful forever, so she stole a drug that she believed would give her youth, beauty, and immortality. However, as she swallowed the drug, she felt herself floating upward. She soared up to the moon where her youth and beauty were preserved, but as punishment for the theft, she was doomed to remain on the moon forever.

And, even to the Chinese, the moon symbolizes romance. Yueh Lao is the old man who lives on the moon, and he is the universal matchmaker. On the night of the harvest moon, he is busily engaged in tying couples together with invisible red silk thread. Young girls have a lot of faith in Yueh Lao. They visit temples to pray for a vision of their future husbands. After burning incense, the girls throw oracle bones before the image of their favorite god, then walk alone at midnight in the direction the bones pointed. They eavesdrop at each door they come to until they overhear a conversation. The first thing they hear is their fortune for the coming year.

Special food for the day is the moon cake, filled and decorated to look round and yellow like the moon. There is a legend about the moon cakes, too. One time there was a plot to overthrow the Chinese government, but the loyal subjects sent secret messages to each other by concealing them in festival cakes exchanged as gifts. So moon cakes became traditional as gifts to carry messages of friendship.

### Double Ten Day

Double Ten Day is Taiwan's biggest national holiday. It commemorates the founding of the Chinese Republic by Dr. Sun Yat-sen, on October 10, 1911. The day is popularly called "Double Ten Day," "10-10 Day," or "Double Tenth Day" because it is the tenth day of the tenth month. Thousands of Chinese who live in other countries return to Taiwan to celebrate that day. Government buildings are gaily decorated and the nationalist Chinese flag flutters from every available point. Many social and sports events are scheduled for that day, and exhibits to show the economic progress the Republic of China has made since 1911 are open to the public. In Taipei, the capital of the Republic of China, a long, precisely organized parade passes before President

Chiang Kai-shek and hundreds of other patriotic officials. During and after the parade, military planes execute breathtakingly rigid military maneuvers.

Other holidays of national significance are Youth Day on March 29; Confucius' birthday, celebrated as Teacher's Day on September 28; Dr. Sun Yat-sen's birthday, as Father of the Republic, on November 12; and Constitution Day on December 25.

### AMIS

In the fall, the aborigines hold their own harvest festival, which is very colorful, with native costumes, dances and displays. The aborigines are descendants of the people who first lived on the island. Since they came from the South Sea Islands, they don't look very much like Chinese. When these people were the only inhabitants, they roamed the island and lived on wild animals, plants, and fruits. They made no effort to increase their food supply, but moved to another location when food became scarce. They were fierce head hunters, so other people who came to the island tried to avoid them.

Today there are only nine tribes of aborigines left, and most of them have settled along the eastern coast. They are no longer unfriendly. One tribe lives near Sun Moon Lake which is a beautiful man-made lake in the mountains of central Taiwan. The largest remaining tribe, the Amis, lives along the eastern coast in beautiful Toroko gorge. They are friendly people and very talented in singing and dancing. During their festival, which lasts three days, they wear bright, colorful, native costumes. They sing, perform folk songs and dances, and exhibit handicrafts. Since they live in the midst of huge marble deposits, they make many unusual objects from marble. They are also proud of their collections of stones in natural, unusual shapes. Their display of orchids is almost unbelievable. They have only recently opened their festival to foreign visitors, and in 1970 more than 30,000 Chinese and visitors from other lands attended.

## Music

Chinese music, especially folk music, is very old and very important to the Chinese way of life. Confucius wrote a book in which he considered music a necessary part of civilized life. Workmen have always sung as they worked, making words and melodies fit their body movements as they planted crops or reaped harvests. From babyhood, children become familiar with songs sung in their homes, in working groups, in children's games, and in stage performances.

The original Chinese musical instruments were made of eight materials found in nature: skin, stone, reeds, metal, clay, wood, bamboo, and gourds. Many of the instruments in use today for classical Chinese renditions are as old as China's history. These instruments do not produce chords with which we are familiar, so the music sounds shrill, harsh, and very different to our ears.

In every neighborhood is a stage to be used for Chinese Opera. Sometimes the plays are merely the story of some honored person's life in the community, and sometimes they are stories about famous people in China's history. And sometimes they are purely fictional with legendary characters. But whatever the play is about, all parts are sung in high pitched falsetto voices accompanied by ancient Chinese musical instruments.

In neighborhoods, the parts are often "made up" as the play progresses, but in the city theatres, the parts are memorized. However, there is always quite a bit of freedom for the actor to change the part as he desires. Such performances, regardless of where they are performed, make up the Chinese national drama known as "Chinese Opera."

Each opera tells a complete story, so it may be very lengthy. Neighborhood operas often last for days, beginning before noon, playing until 10 P.M., and continuing the next day.

Chinese Opera is colorful to both the eye and the ear. It combines music, dance, pantomime, and strenuous acrobatics. Even though all of the roles are sung, the performance is often so colorful and impressive that the music may be overlooked. Plays are emotional and profound. The ones given in opera houses are often hundreds of years old.

There is very little scenery, so every gesture of the actor is important and symbolic. Special attention must be given to sleeve, hand, and foot movements, and the actor must be very skillful in these manipulations. If an actor comes striding onto the stage carrying a riding whip, that means he is riding a horse. If he throws the whip on the floor, it means he got off the horse. He may hold his hands at arm's length then bring them together slowly to indicate closing a door; a girl may dismiss her lover in the same manner. An actor's walk tells of his character. A high official clumps across the stage, but a beautiful girl glides across. A clown has manners and gestures all his own.

Costumes are very bright, elaborate, and from the Ming Dynasty (about 1368) regardless of the period in history to which the story belongs. Costumes also indicate the class to which the character belongs; such as rulers, generals, scholars, servants, and others. Color also shows rank, status, and personal character.

Heavily painted faces are another unusual feature. The designs and color identify the role of the wearer. Red means the character is loyal and brave, a black faces means he is honest, green has an ethereal meaning of spirits, gold is for gods, and a clown's nose is always white.

The musicans sit at the side of the stage keeping time with clackers, and marking climaxes with a clang of cymbals. They accompany the falsetto voices of the soloists with the eerie sounds of the ancient Chinese instruments, and intensify emotional scenes.

## Art

Many present day Chinese artists are using Western techniques, but the spirit is still oriental. Chinese painters start, as all Chinese have for more than 2,000 years, by imitating a master painter. They paint mountains, streams, birds, and flowers in a typically Chinese way. The paintings have a mystic quality of lightness, yet have little perspective. Chinese brush-painting produces pictures similar to watercolors.

Caligraphy, the writing of Chinese characters with a brush, is a form of brush-painting. It is an art form of its own, much like a fine type of handwriting. It is not merely elegant penmanship, but an artistic product of an individual. The calligraphy of famous masters is readily recognizable because of individual characteristics. It has been practiced by both scholars and artists in China for centuries, and was at one time considered to be the mark of a gentleman. Calligraphers often write poems on the face of paintings as literary complements to the picture. Paintings and examples of fine calligraphy are customary gifts of esteem.

## Language

Chinese is spoken, as a native language, by more people than any other language in the world.

Down through the years spoken Chinese has changed,

as any living language does. One change has come about
through the development of dialects in different regions of
the country. Even though all dialects came from the same
basic language, today many of them can't be understood from
one region to another. So, just because a person speaks
Chinese does not mean he can be understood any place in
China. To try to simplify this, the government has declared
the Mandarin dialect to be the official language of modern
China. Mandarin is taught in schools and used on all official
occasions. As a result, fewer people are now using their
regional dialects, and Mandarin is gaining in popularity,
especially among the younger people.

Written Chinese, with its picture characters, looks very
difficult but it is interesting to know how it originated.
Thousands of years ago Chinese people drew pictures to send
messages. It was from these pictures that the standardized
characters developed. Learning to read and write the characters is not difficult if you know their origins and the idea
behind them.

For instance:

木  looks like a tree, so it means "tree."

木 木  looks like two trees, so it means "forest."

However, since characters can't always be put together to
make other words, as the letters of our alphabet can, it is
necessary to learn thousands of characters. This requires a
lot of study and memory work. In order to read newspapers,
a person must know about 2000 characters, and it takes
thousands more if a person wants to go to college.

Chinese read rows of characters from top to bottom
across the page from right to left. To read a book or magazine,
they begin at the upper righthand corner of the back page,

and read down, moving to the next line on the left. They follow the same system on each page until they come to the lower lefthand corner of the front page to finish the book.

Speak the following words of Mandarin by following these rules, and any Mandarin-speaking Chinese can understand you:

Pronounce every "a" as in *father*; every "e" as in *them*; and every "i" like the "ee" in *seem*.

Pronounce EVERY letter. Two vowels pronounced one after the other quickly will sound like one, but both are pronounced. For instance, "ai" will sound like a long "i" as in *Taiwan*, and "ei" will sound like a long "a" as in *Taipei*.

Try to pronounce the following words, and use them with your friends.

Tsao (t-s-ow) ........................ good morning
Ni hao ma? (knee how ma?) ...... good afternoon,
                                        or how are you?
Tsai chen (t-s-i chen) .. .. .. .. .. .. .. good bye
Hsieh hsieh (shey shey) ................. thank you
Hen hao (hen how) ....................very good
Pu hao (boo how) .............. not good (very bad)

You may be interested in learning to read, write, and speak numbers in Chinese. See next page.

### Name Chops

A chop is a piece of hard material in the shape of a small stick that has a person's name carved into one end of it. For thousands of years it has been used in China as a signature. The chop is pressed onto a cake of colored wax, or ink pad, then onto paper to make an imprint, Any person may have his name carved on a chop, but it can be used as an official signature on legal documents only if it has been

| English | Character | Chinese |
|---|---|---|
| One | 一 | i (ē) or (ee) |
| Two | 二 | erh (er) |
| Three | 三 | san (sän) |
| Four | 四 | ssu ("u" like "o" in look) |
| Five | 五 | wu (woo) |
| Six | 六 | liu (li-oo) |
| Seven | 七 | chi (chee) |
| Eight | 八 | pa (ba) |
| Nine | 九 | chiu (chew) |
| Ten | 十 | shih (sher) |
| Eleven | 十一 | shih-i |
| Twenty-three | 二十三 | erh-shih-san |
| Fifty-six | 五十六 | wu-shih-liu |

registered with the government. Official chops always are used with red ink or wax.

Chops of ivory, bamboo, soapstone, or metal are common today. However, in ancient times, jade, the symbol of nobility, was the favorite material. People of wealth often used other semiprecious stones and had handles elaborately carved with their family crests. The sculpture on the handle indicated social position or professional status.

A chop maker must be a good penman, a careful engraver,

and a fine artist. The value of a modern chop depends on the material from which it is made, and the reputation of the craftsman who made it. The value of an old chop depends on the material from which it is made, its age, its past ownership, and its role in Chinese history. Wealthy Chinese collect ancient chops as a hobby.

## Education

Almost everyone in Taiwan can read and write, and many have college educations. There is free, compulsory education through the ninth grade. The school attendance rate is second highest in all Asia. New schools are being built rapidly, and there are now enough classrooms for every student above the second grade to attend school all day.

Pupils in public schools wear uniforms and carry bags on their shoulders for their books.

In addition to the usual studies—reading, writing, arithmetic, history, science, and geography—world culture and fine arts are important. School bands, including all regular musical instruments, are standard for both junior and senior high schools. Vocational courses are also part of the junior and senior high schools. Physical education is provided in all schools from first grade to college, and many schools have sports teams.

School buildings are of modern design with wide balconies that provide light, air, and protection from rainfall, which is often heavy. Boys and girls, after primary school, have separate classes. Teachers are highly respected, and they insist on strict attention at all times. The school day is long, beginning about eight o'clock and lasting until after four o'clock in the afternoon. However, the strict concentration and long hours are broken by outdoor physical activities.

In 1968 Taiwan had ten universities, seventy-five separate colleges, and fourteen military institutions, all granting degrees. Technical institutes are teaching nuclear science and electronics. The National School of the Arts and the Taiwan School of Nursing are both located in Taipei. Doctorates may be earned in economics, political science, literature, and medicine.

One-fourth of all the people who live in Taiwan are enrolled in some kind of school, so everyone is busy studying or working. Adult education classes are offered at night in public school buildings, where a person can study formal educational subjects, or vocations. Art, sewing and pattern making, and English classes are popular.

Every city has at least one library. The Chinese believe that all things come through education, and education is acquired through books, so libraries are important and highly esteemed. Newspapers, magazines, and books are available at book stores or may be delivered to the house. TV is expanding since Taipei has its own station, and radio reaches into most homes.

## Religion

Religious freedom is guaranteed by the constitution, and people practice any religion they choose. Taoism, Buddhism, and Christianity are all active religions on the island. Both Catholic and Protestant groups take active parts in the welfare of the people. All are cooperative. In 1964, seven different religions joined in a display of their sacred books, utensils, and pictures. Nearly half a million people visited the unusual exhibit.

Buddhism is known as a religion of love, peace, and "the middle road." Taoism has been called the religion of inaction because it does not really oppose anything. Many Chinese don't know the difference between the two religions, so it isn't important.

Confucius was China's most famous teacher and philosopher, but he was not a deity or god. His teachings are known and quoted today, and his birthday is celebrated every year. He wrote books and gave people many quotations to live by, although he didn't say many of the things people attribute to him today. Confucianism is a way of life, not a religion.

The first Presbyterian missionary came to Taiwan in 1865, and in 1965 twenty-two Protestant churches joined in observing their centennial. Catholic priests came to Taiwan in 1626, but their church has grown only in recent years. Both Catholics and Protestants operate hospitals, clinics, universities, and private schools.

Temples hold a very important place in Chinese culture. On Taiwan there are 2913 Buddhist temples and shrines with 350 of them dedicated to the goddess of mercy. There are 2000 Taoist temples; and hundreds of others are dedicated to local deities not connected with Buddhism or Taoism.

Lungshan Temple (Dragon Hill), located in Taipei, is the oldest and most famous Buddhist temple on the island. Its stone pillars are hand-carved, and the elaborate roof with its turned-up corners is brilliant with figures and symbols painted in bright colors and gold. Periodically, the roof and exterior is cleaned and painted. Inside are many statues and altars dedicated to the goddess of mercy.

Legend explains that the corners of the roof are turned up to keep evil spirits away. They say that when the evil spirits come down and try to sneak in from above, they slide back up the steep corners and are plummeted into the sky. This protection can't be guaranteed, but the graceful, turned-up corners are attractive, interesting, and typically Chinese.

# 4

# CITIES

Over 1,600,000 people live in Taipei, the largest city in Taiwan. It is located in the northern part of the island. It is the capital of the Republic of China, the home of President Chiang Kai-shek. Near the center of the city is the big, red brick presidential office building, the university hospital, and the Botanical Gardens. The streets are lined with small shops, each specializing in one type of merchandise. There are very few large department stores, but they are popular. Taipei is a very noisy city with screeching bicycles, speeding motorcycles, honking taxis, and crowds of people.

Before 1968, pedicabs were used as taxis and for hauling all kinds of loads. The pedicab is a bicycle with a one-seated covered buggy mounted behind in place of the back wheel. The taxi fare was bargained for before the ride. The pedicab used for hauling had small closed, or open, truck beds attached instead of the buggy. Because pedicabs were used for so many different things and for such heavy loads, Taiwan was often referred to as a "leg-powered island." However, as automotive traffic increased, pedicabs became more and more unreliable and dangerous. In 1968, the government passed a law making them illegal.

In the Botanical Gardens are national buildings surrounded by tropical and subtropical plants. The National Historical Museum boasts typical Chinese architecture with large red pillars, stone lions at the entrance, and a big red lacquer door. Inside this building it is possible to follow the entire history of China in its displays and exhibits.

The National Science Hall is a round building patterned after the Hall of Heaven in Peiping, on the China mainland It contains models and exhibits of scientific interest.

The National Arts Hall is used for concerts, stage dramas, operas, and other performances. It is a very popular building and is in use almost every day and evening.

The National Library is of great importance and interest to the Chinese people. Books, educational material, and teachers are held in the highest esteem, so the people take great pride in their libraries.

The new National Palace Museum is located in a scenic suburb northwest of Taipei. It is nestled in the foothills of Yangmingshan (Grass Mountain) and is surrounded by low, tree-covered hills which afford protection. Inside the beautiful marble building are 240,000 pieces of China's great art treasures. The art objects cover 6,000 years of Chinese history. The precious objects on display are secured in special glass cases to protect them from earthquake damage. They are constantly being changed because only 3,600 can be displayed at one time.

In 1965, when the new building was completed, the art treasures were moved from buildings and caves in central Taiwan. Visitors come from all over the world to view and study the art work of China, and many curators from the United States have pursued research projects there.

### Central Taiwan

Taichung is the second largest city in Taiwan and is located near the center of the island. It is the provincial (state) capital of Taiwan. The capital was moved there when Taipei became the capital of the Republic of China, so the buildings are all new. They are white, very modern buildings that show Western influence in architecture. All government assemblies are housed in this area on the outskirts of Taichung, and a little village, Chung-shing, has grown up around them.

On a hilltop a few miles south of Taichung is the largest Buddha in the Far East. It is made of black material, has a large red stone in the center of its forhead, and is guarded by two huge marble lions. A person may enter the statue to explore a small museum in its base, then climb a stairway up into its head to view the countryside through its eyes.

The highest mountain peak, Yu Shan (Mt. Morrison), is also near the center of Taiwan. It is a favorite spot for mountain climbers.

Hualien, the largest city on the eastern coast of north central Taiwan, has an airport and is the starting point of the breathtaking Pacific Precipice Highway which has been carved from a marble wall of Toroko Gorge. Its southern terminal is Suao, near Taitung, which is the target of many typhoons.

## Southern Taiwan

Tainan, the oldest city in Taiwan, is located at the southern end of the island, where the climate is tropical. Three centuries ago Tainan was the capital of Taiwan, and still has many historical landmarks. The temple built in memory of the leader, Cheng Cheng-kung (Koxinga), who expelled the Dutch from Taiwan is located in Tainan.

Kaohsiung, Taiwan's busiest seaport, is near Tainan, two hundred miles from Taipei. It is the industrial center of the island and is the site of Taiwan's only oil refinery. Near Kaohsiung is a new area made from reclaimed land that is attracting a great deal of attention. Flowing through this industrial city is the romantic "River of Love," and nearby is Cheng Ching lake with its bridge of nine turns. The bridge was built with many sharp and sudden offsets, or turns, to keep evil spirits, who can travel only in straight lines, from crossing. Kaohsiung can be reached from the northern tip of the island by air-conditioned, diesel express trains, or by planes. The extreme southern tip of the island with its lighthouse is only a few miles south of Kaohsiung.

# 5

# HOBBIES AND SPORTS

## Handicrafts

Taiwan handicrafts have won prizes at more than fifty international fairs, and Chinese are known all over the world for their handmade articles. Their lifelike wooden carvings are unique and represent many Chinese legends. Statues are usually carved from camphor wood and are hand polished.

One well-loved statue is of an old man holding his fishing line in his right hand so it falls over his shoulder as he carries a fish in his left hand. He has a long, finely carved beard, wears a hat with a hole in it to slip over his topknot, and is barefooted. He represents good luck because, as the story goes, he went fishing without any equipment to catch fish. He just bent a pin, tied it to a line, and without even any bait, hung it in the water and caught a fish! Now, how could he have done that if not with luck?

Chinese are expert tailors. They don't use patterns for cutting clothing. They measure an individual, study the picture of the garment he wants, and draw the pattern on the material to the customer's exact size. This is the reason Chinese clothes fit so nicely.

Chinese ceramics, such as teapots, drum stools (copied after those used in the Imperial Palace), vases, and table lamps are intricately designed and hand-carved. The article is cast in a mold, using a special type of clay, and allowed to dry partially. Then it is removed from the mold and either hand-painted, or stenciled for cut-out designs. All-over designs are cut out with tiny knives before they are ready to be fired. Art lovers and visitors from all over the world enjoy visiting the ceramics factories to watch and admire these special skills.

Thick woolen Chinese rugs are manufactured in Taiwan. The wool is imported, but the rugs are designed and hand-tied in small factories in Taiwan. One square foot of rug contains 8000 to 9000 knots, and one person can tie 10,000 knots in one day. Most of the work is done by young people, but the designing and supervision is done by experienced men. Rugs are also made from a native plant, similar to flax, called "*ramie.*" *Ramie* rugs are durable and moth-proof.

Hand carving of marble is a more recently developed handicraft, but is becoming very popular. The articles include vases, boxes, trays, bowls, sets of dishes, and worry-stones. Worry-stones are small, smooth, curved pieces of marble a person can carry in his pocket to rub when he is nervous or worried. Marble benches, table tops, bathroom fixtures, and door knobs are made from white, black, green, or gray marble.

Dolls are in every handicraft shop. They represent characters in Chinese folklore, display costumes of various religions and classes, and portray famous historic figures. Dolls are made in various sizes, but small ones usually show provincial differences in clothing or work habits.

For centuries the art of embroidery has been part of the education of Chinese girls and boys. Chinese embroider tablecloths, napkins, and pillow cases in such a typical manner that they can be recognized any place in the world as Chinese handwork. Pictures embroidered on silk, satin, and brocade are typically Chinese in design and workmanship.

### Firecrackers

Hundreds of years ago the Chinese invented firecrackers, and even today they use more of them than any other nation. Their firecrackers are small, but are bound together in long strings so the noise increases as they explode. For celebrations, strings of firecrackers are hung from the edges of roofs, from trees, or from especially constructed frameworks. They are hung to celebrate weddings, birthdays, moving into a new house, election results, special honors, and anything of importance. After the strings have been hung, someone lights the bottom firecracker at a designated time, and everyone cheers and claps as the pop-pop-popping travels to the top. If the occasion is important enough, there may be several strings. With so many people living in Taiwan, there is always something to celebrate so the noise of firecrackers is a familiar sound.

There are small shops that sell only firecrackers the entire year.

### Stamps

Two thousand years ago China used a system of pony stations to send messages. It was customary to attach a symbol to a message to indicate its importance and the speed required for its delivery. A slightly burned rooster feather attached to a message meant it was urgent. A message with the feather attached could be carried two hundred miles in twenty four hours.

Private letter-carrying began in the fifteenth century but at that time there were no postage stamps. In 1878 China issued its first stamps. In 1894 the first commemorative stamps were issued, and the first stamps issued by the Chinese Imperial Post were offered in 1897.

Philately is very popular in Taiwan where there are an estimated 100,000 collectors. Students, servicemen, and people in professional careers make up most of the interested persons. In addition to the China Philatelic Society in Taipei, there are dozens of local clubs. At least six newspapers carry daily philatelic columns, and the various clubs publish regular bulletins through magazines. A complete catalog of Chinese stamps from 1878 to 1957 has been published in Chinese and English, and supplements are issued annually. The Directorate General of Posts has been active in helping domestic and foreign collectors.

The famous insect and orchid stamps were chosen by LIFE magazine in February, 1960, as among the world's most beautiful stamps. Four ancient Chinese paintings (seventh to eleventh centuries) have been reproduced on stamps in their original colors. One of these, "Two Horses and A Groom," was used on the cover of the September, 1960, issue of London's *Stamp Magazine*. Eighteen art treasure stamps, including reproductions of bronze, porcelain, and jade pieces, are being issued in batches of three.

Chinese stamp collectors are as anxious as any others in the world to trade stamps.

### Scouting

The first Boy Scout troop in the Republic of China was organized in 1912, and girl scouting was established ten years later. Several national jamborees have been held in China, but the largest was the fourth one, held in northern Taiwan in 1970. More than 14,700 boys and girls, including overseas Chinese and foreigners from ten countries attended. Boys and girls joined in opening ceremonies, then pitched their own separate camps.

In Taiwan the scout movement is so highly thought of that training is given in public schools, although membership is voluntary. Schools own camping equipment and sponsor several outings a year. Students may borrow tents and other camping equipment from the school. Scout leaders receive special training at Taiwan National University, and President Chiang Kai-shek is a strong backer of scouting.

## Sports

Probably the most popular sports in Taiwan are baseball, basketball, and swimming, but the Chinese like and enjoy all sports. The people of Taiwan are proud of their Little League baseball team, which won the world championship at Williamsport, Pennsylvania, in 1969. Men and boys practice catching balls whenever they have free time, and it is common to see them outside office buildings at lunchtime tossing balls back and forth.

Track and field events are popular and Taiwan has had some outstanding athletes entered in world competitions. They play soccer instead of football, and volleyball is popular for girls. Chinese men are very interested in body-building techniques such as judo, weight lifting, and shadowboxing. Golf is the businessman's game, but it is gaining in popularity with all.

## Health

Taiwan is the only place certified by the World Health Organization as having wiped out malaria. Diseases, such as tuberculosis, cholera, smallpox, and polio are found less and less often. Medical groups and religious organizations have been very successful with vaccinations.

No one in Taiwan needs to be without medical care. Many families have health insurance, and those who don't have it and can't pay for private care, can go to a government hospital. There are about 200 hospitals and over 600 health centers. In Taipei, in addition to the National Taiwan University Hospital, there are Presbyterian and Seventh Day Adventist sponsored hospitals, and many smaller ones.

The American Bureau for Medical Aid to China (AB-MAC) has been active for thirty-three years. One of its most noteworthy advances has been the care of mothers and babies. This has been followed closely by child health care.

Polio, which in the past crippled thousands of children, has been almost wiped out through the efforts of the Maryknoll Sisters, who have administered vaccine.

Not only does all this make Taiwan one of the most healthful places in Asia to live, but its spectacular scenery and pleasant way of life make this "beautiful island" one of the nicest places in the world.

# INDEX